Let's say the Grace together

Exploring a trilogy of blessing

Derek Prime

ISBN 0 902548 55 7

Published by Day One Publications
6 Sherman Road, Bromley, Kent BR1 3JH

Front Cover photo: Grasmere by A. and D. Vincent

Designed and printed by Clifford Frost Ltd, Wimbledon SW19 2SE

Contents

Introduction

Which is the most quoted verse in the Bible? Probably our immediate response is to think of John 3:16: 'For God so loved the world that he gave his one and only Son, that whoever believes in him shall not perish but have eternal life.' Certainly in evangelism that verse comes top.

A second suggestion might be the opening words of 'the Lord's Prayer' – 'Our Father in heaven, hallowed be your name' (Matthew 6:9). But not every part of the Christian Church regularly uses the Lord's Prayer in its corporate worship.

There is, however, a prayer at the end of Paul's second letter to the Corinthians that all parts of the Christian Church – so far as I can discover – frequently employ: 'May the grace of the Lord Jesus Christ, and the love of God, and the fellowship of the Holy Spirit be with you all' (13:14). It is difficult to discover for how long this has been a practice. Paul may have ended his letter with these words because they were already a familiar prayer of the early Christians. It is not surprising that the prayer appeared in the Elizabethan Prayer Book in England in 1559 as part of the Litany, and then in Morning and Evening Prayer in the Prayer Book of 1662.

In many churches it is customary for ministers to use these words as a closing prayer, but in recent decades it has also become the practice for believers to say them together, in response to the invitation, 'Let's say the grace together!'

They are familiar words, but what do they mean? What do we understand by them? For what are we praying? What justification is there for this being one of the most used prayers of the Christian Church worldwide?   To answer these questions is our purpose.   To know something of the answers helps us to grow immeasurably in our knowledge of God.

The prayer divides naturally into three parts.   It is important that once we have looked at each part separately that we discern the relationship of the three together.   Let us then explore this trilogy of blessing, for that is what it is!

Part One

Chapter One

The Grace of the Lord Jesus Christ

Grace is one of the loveliest words in a Christian's vocabulary. It was a term I seldom, if ever, used in my pre-Christian days. But since I became a Christian, it has been frequently on my lips and in my thoughts, especially when I join in praise, prayer and conversation with other Christians. It is the expression above all others which sums up God's amazing work of salvation for me a guilty sinner. I have been saved by grace – and by grace alone.

Christians were not the first people to employ the word grace, but they seem to have been the first to use it in the sense in which we now understand it. Originally among the Greeks grace had in view that which gives pleasure or joy. But then it came to have this deeper dimension in its use by Christians: grace is unmerited favour. Its link with the original meaning of grace is significant: nothing gives Christians greater joy than appreciating that their salvation depends wholly upon what God has done for them in Jesus Christ rather than upon anything they do or need to do to earn it.

Grace is God's wonderful kindness – the sort of kindness that takes our breath away, and is the source of unique joy and pleasure. Grace is God's sovereign kindness at work – His acting in ways open to Him alone. It is His favour to totally undeserving men and women like ourselves.

A distinctive quality

Grace's uniqueness is that it cannot be earned or deserved. The parable Jesus told of the lost son illustrates this perfectly (Luke 15:11-24). The son makes a complete mess of his life. He not only squanders the wealth he persuaded his father to let him have, but he ends up so impoverished that the only job he can get is that of feeding pigs, and he is so hungry that he even envies them their food.   But through his dire circumstances, he comes to himself.   As he makes his weary way home, he rehearses the speech of regret and repentance he will make to his father, recognising that at best he can hope for an employee's role in his father's household.

But he is in for a big surprise!   Before he catches sight of his father, his father sees him from a long way off – he has been daily looking for his return.   Filled with compassion for his son, the father runs out to meet him, throws his arms around him, and kisses him.   The son begins to make his prepared speech, but the father calls for the best robe, for a ring to be placed on his son's finger and sandals on his feet.   He caps it all by calling for a feast to celebrate his son's return.   All of these benefits were sheer grace – and so too are the blessings God gives us through the grace of our Lord Jesus Christ!

Our Lord Jesus Christ's coming into the world proves that grace cannot be merited.   How could we ever deserve not only His coming into the world, but His dying for our sins?   As Paul reminds us, 'You know the grace of our Lord Jesus Christ, that though he was rich, yet for your sakes he became poor, so that you through his poverty might become rich' (2 Corinthians 8:9). Grace is the only word Paul finds anywhere near adequate to describe such a mind-boggling concept as the Lord of glory becoming poor to make us rich.

As we get to know someone well, features of that person's character soon stand out, and make an impression upon us which we seldom forget.   That was the experience of the apostles and first disciples with regard to Jesus.   They lived with Him, ate and drank with Him, watched Him when He was tired and exhausted; in fact, they fully shared His daily life.   As a consequence they were in no doubt as to what impressed them most in those three years, for they declared, 'The Word became flesh and lived for a while among us.   We have seen his glory, the glory of the one and only Son, who came from the Father, full of grace and truth' (John 1:14). Jesus' life was *full of grace.* 'The law was given by Moses: *grace* and truth came through Jesus Christ' (John 1:17). God gives us His grace through the Lord Jesus (1 Corinthians 1:4): He is the door for us into the riches of that grace.

John Bunyan's words concerning the grace of the Lord Jesus Christ, although in quaint language to our ears, are worth pondering until we say them with the same warmth and thankfulness:

> *'Thou Son of the Blessed,*
> *what grace was manifested in Thy condescension.*
> *Grace brought Thee down from Heaven;*
> *grace stripped Thee of Thy glory;*
> *grace made Thee poor and despised;*
> *grace made Thee bear such burdens of sin,*
> > *such burdens of sorrow,*
> > *such burdens of God's curse as are unspeakable.*
> *O Son of God!*
> *Grace was in all Thy tears;*
> > *grace came out of Thy side with Thy blood;*
> > *grace came forth with every word of*
> > *Thy sweet mouth;*
> > *grace came out where the whip smote Thee,*
> > *where the thorn pricked Thee.*
> *Here is grace indeed!*
> *Grace to make angels wonder,*
> > *grace to make sinners happy,*
> > *grace to astonish devils.'*

God's nearness to help

One often forgotten expression of God's grace is His nearness and readiness to help us at those moments when we appreciate how totally unworthy we are of His aid. As our Lord Jesus Christ exercised His ministry during those three significant years in Palestine, His grace was seen in the manner in which He was always available to help those who knew – or came to see – that they deserved no help.

The woman of Samaria was thirsty for the quenching of her inner thirst that no well of ordinary water ever satisfied. She had tried the empty waters of the world – the wells of sexual desire and worldly enjoyment. Jesus showed that He knew everything about her when He replied to her protestation that she had no husband, 'You are right when you say you have no husband. The fact is, you have had five husbands, and the man you now have is not your husband. What you have just said is quite true' (John 4:17). Jesus then brought her to a knowledge of salvation as she believed in Him, and in some sense at least it was for her sake He 'had to go through Samaria' (John 4:4).

Zacchaeus, the cheating tax-collector of Jericho, also discovered that Jesus was at hand to help, although most others would have had no time for him. Jesus entered Jericho and was passing through (Luke 19:1-10). He reached the place where Zacchaeus was hiding up a sycamore tree, unknown to others probably, but not to Jesus. Jesus halted and demonstrated His concern for Zacchaeus' salvation. He did not stop at that, but entered his home in order to assure him of his new-found relationship with God.

At the time of the crucifixion all the penitent thief hoped for at best was that Jesus might remember him when He came into His kingdom. He discovered the wonder of Jesus' grace in that he was promised nearness to Jesus in paradise that day (Luke 23:42,43)! In a moment a dying thief who trusted Jesus in the last hours of his life was given the assurance of a whole eternity of happiness. Such is the grace of the Lord Jesus Christ!

Jesus Christ's closeness, especially when we know we do not deserve Him to be near us, is a meaningful and practical expression of His grace, and not least when we realise He is present as our Helper and Deliverer. This is a vital truth to which to cling when our consciences – and the enemy of souls – may rightly tell us that we do not deserve either Jesus' presence or help. That may be true, but all such grounds of rejection are overcome by grace!

Expression in song

It is little wonder that grace has captured the imagination of hymn and song writers!   Philip Doddridge wrote,

> *'Grace! 'tis a charming sound,*
> *Harmonious to the ear:*
> *Heaven with the echo shall resound,*
> *And all the earth shall hear.'*

Samuel Davies expresses his own sense of wonder,

> *'Great God of wonders, all Thy ways*
> *Are matchless, godlike and divine;*
> *But the fair glories of Thy grace*
> *More godlike and unrivalled shine:*
>
> *Who is a pardoning God like Thee?*
> *Or who has grace so rich and free?'*

Or, more well known still, we have John Newton's hymn,

> *'Amazing grace!   how sweet the sound*
> *That saved a wretch like me;*
> *I once was lost, but now am found;*
> *Was blind, but now I see.'*

To be born again of God's Spirit is to have our eyes opened to grace, and its inexhaustible riches in Jesus Christ.   The emphasis in this familiar prayer of 2 Corinthians 13:14 is upon this first part because it is through the grace of the Lord Jesus that we discover the Father's love and the Spirit's fellowship. Significantly the words, 'The grace of the Lord Jesus Christ be with you' occur on their own in the New Testament (1 Corinthians 16:23; Philippians 4:23; Philemon 25; Revelation 22:21) whereas the other parts do not.

Chapter Two

The Grace of Jesus Christ's forgiveness

For centuries Christians have employed the words 'The grace of the Lord Jesus Christ be with you' either as a greeting or as a parting prayer.   In asking for this threefold blessing in 2 Corinthians 13:14, Jesus Christ's grace is the first blessing from God we seek.   It would not be wrong to reverse the order, but there is an appropriateness about this pattern of prayer for blessing since our experience of God's salvation all began with our tasting the grace of the Lord Jesus Christ (1 Peter 2:3; cf. Psalm 34:8).

It was not until we understood our Saviour's grace that we entered into a personal experience of God's love and the Holy Spirit's fellowship.   The first lesson we learnt about salvation was that it is through the grace of the Lord Jesus that we are saved (Acts 15:11).   'By grace you have been saved,' the New Testament constantly reminds us.   And the first consequence of that grace of salvation was the forgiveness of our sins.

Everywhere in the Bible – in the Old Testament as well as in the New – forgiveness is the first blessing of salvation.   Psalm 103 is unique in the Old Testament for providing a shop-window of salvation's benefits, and it gives first place to the forgiveness of our sins: 'Praise the Lord, O my soul, and forget not all his benefits.   He forgives all my sins ...' (Psalm 103:2,3).   David speaks of the blessedness of those who know that their sins are forgiven (Psalm 32:1).

A prominent miracle in the early days of Jesus' public ministry was the healing of a paralysed man let down through the roof by his enterprising and believing friends.   Instead of telling the man first to take up his bed and walk, Jesus rather said to him, 'Son, your sins are forgiven you', indicating that no matter how great his physical distress may have been, the need of his soul for forgiveness was greater (Matthew 9:2; Mark 2:5).

The apostle Peter was privileged to declare the gospel for the first time to Gentiles when at God's command he arrived at the home of Cornelius. The climax of his presentation of the gospel and his preaching of Jesus was to say, 'All the prophets testify about him that everyone who believes in him receives forgiveness of sins through his name' (Acts 10:43).

Through the grace of the Lord Jesus in dying for us, we are delivered from sin's guilt and penalty. He stood in our place, the righteous for the unrighteous, to bring us to God (1 Peter 3:18). On account of His atoning work, we have been acquitted from all charges against us of disobedience to God's Law, and we are reckoned righteous in God's sight – and all through His grace. As the old acrostic based on the five letters of the word G-R-A-C-E expresses it, we know *God's Riches At Christ's Expense.*

John Bunyan captures well the Christian's first understanding of forgiveness through the grace of the Lord Jesus in the experience of Pilgrim in his *Pilgrim's Progress* when he comes to the Cross and loses his burden there. Bunyan writes, 'Now I saw in my dream that the highway, up which Christian was to go, was fenced on either side with a wall, and that wall was called Salvation (Isaiah 26:1). Up this way, therefore, did burdened Christian run, but not without great difficulty, because of the load on his back.

'He ran thus till he came at a place somewhat ascending; and upon that place stood a Cross, and a little below, in the bottom, a Sepulchre. So I saw in my dream, that just as Christian came up with the Cross, his burden loosed from off his shoulders, and fell from off his back, and began to tumble, and so continued to do, till it came to the mouth of the Sepulchre, where it fell in, and I saw it no more.

'Then was Christian glad and lightsome, and said, with a merry heart, He hath given me rest by his sorrow and life by his death.   Then he stood still a while to look and wonder; for it was very surprising to him that the sight of the Cross should thus ease him of his burden.   He looked, therefore, and looked again, even till the springs that were in his head sent the waters down his cheeks (Zechariah 12:10). ... Christian gave three leaps for joy, and went on singing.

"Blest Cross!   blest Sepulchre!   blest rather be
The Man that there was put to shame for me ..." '

Bunyan describes every Christian's experience.   Through the grace of Jesus Christ in His atoning death for us, we are forgiven, and eased of our burden of sin.   Charles Wesley expresses the same glorious deliverance in his delightful hymn 'And can it be that I should gain an interest in the Saviour's blood?'   He writes,

'Long my imprisoned spirit lay
Fast bound in sin and nature's night;
Thine eye diffused a quickening ray -
I woke, the dungeon flamed with light;
My chains fell off, my heart was free.
I rose, went forth and followed Thee.

'No condemnation now I dread;
Jesus, and all in Him, is mine!
Alive in Him, my living Head,
And clothed in righteousness divine,
Bold I approach the eternal throne,
And claim the crown, through Christ, my own.'

No wonder Bunyan's Pilgrim jumped three times up into the air with joy!

A necessary reminder

Sadly, we do not stop sinning when we enter into God's salvation through the grace of our Lord Jesus Christ.   We certainly do not sin as before, but we still transgress.   The power of sin is broken in our lives but not our experience of sin.   Whereas once we loved sin in many of its forms, we now hate it.   But so often we find ourselves doing what we hate, and cry, as Paul did, 'What a wretched man I am!' (Romans 7:24).

I remember as a young Christian looking at the man who pointed me to faith in the Lord Jesus, who was twenty years or so older than I, and thinking, 'When I get to his stage in life and Christian growth, I will not have such a battle against sin.'   But I was wrong!   The battle becomes no less as we grow older. Rather the truth is that the conflict becomes more acute because of our increased awareness of God's character, and especially of His holiness.   That makes sense when we remember that the closer we are to a light, the darker is our own shadow.   If we are away from a light, we have no shadow, but the closer we get to it the darker our shadow becomes.   God is light, and the closer we come to Him the more aware we become of our own sinfulness.

We see this truth reflected in Paul's letters.   One of the first New Testament letters he wrote was to the Corinthians, in which he described himself as 'the least of the apostles' (1 Corinthians 15:9).   Later in his ministry, writing to the Ephesians, he speaks of himself as 'the least of all God's people' (Ephesians 3:8). Towards the end of his life, writing to Timothy, he calls himself 'the worst of sinners' (1 Timothy 1:16).   This was not Paul going backwards in Christian experience – as it might at first sight imply – but rather his going forward.   Growing in his knowledge of God through the Lord Jesus, he was closer to the Light, and his shadow was darker.

A daily experience of forgiveness

Our predicament calls, therefore, for a day by day experience of our Lord Jesus Christ's grace.   We need restoring and renewing. We require regular cleansing.   A wonder of our salvation is that through our Saviour's grace God has made provision for exactly this.   While once – before we were reconciled to God – His throne was a throne of judgment, rightly to be feared, now it is a throne of grace, where we may obtain grace to help in our time of need (Hebrews 4:16).   God dispenses His forgiveness of our sins in accordance with the riches of His grace (Ephesians 1:7). Through the merits of our Saviour's once for all sacrifice for our sins, we may know His grace in daily forgiveness.

The Lord Jesus gave a delightful illustration of what we are to understand about daily cleansing and forgiveness in His washing of the disciples' feet (John 13:1-17). Sitting at the table in preparation for their celebration of the Passover, Jesus took them by surprise as He stripped Himself of His outer garments, placed a towel around His waist, and proceeded to wash their feet. When He came to Peter, Peter initially refused to let Him wash his feet. Jesus' answer was, 'Unless I wash you, you have no part with me' (13:8). ' "Then, Lord," Simon Peter replied, "not just my feet but my hands and my head as well!" Jesus answered, "A person who has had a bath needs only to wash his feet; his whole body is clean. And you are clean ..." ' (13:9,10).

The initial experience of salvation is like a bath in which all our sins are forgiven and we are completely cleansed. But thereafter our 'feet' get dirty and need to be washed. The picture is simple yet effective. If we visit Jerusalem we will inevitably visit the Old City, and go down into the busy streets of its shops and markets. Before we leave our hotel or guest house in the morning we will shower or bath. Walking through the Old City in our sandals, our feet will become dirty, and by the time we return to where we are staying for lunch or dinner we will feel that we need to wash our feet, even though we do not need a complete bath. So it is with us in our life in the world. We cannot 'walk' through daily life in the world without our 'feet' becoming 'dirty', without our spoiling our relationship with God through sin in a variety of ways. We do not need to be converted all over again – like having a bath – but we do need to be cleansed from those sins we have committed – that is to say, have our feet washed. As often as our 'feet' are dirty – which happens everyday in some way or other – we need to be cleansed. This benefit is precisely what God promises through the grace of His dear Son. What His Son accomplished on the Cross is relevant not just to my past sins, but to those of the present and the future.

The immediate danger might be to become presumptuous about Jesus Christ's grace of forgiveness, and to take it for granted – or, worse, to think that sin does not matter if it is so easily forgiven and cleansed.   But the grace of the Lord Jesus has the opposite effect; it is certainly not a grace that makes us free to sin.   We cannot suggest, 'Shall we go on sinning, so that grace may increase?' (Romans 6:1).   Rather our experience of this grace of daily cleansing turns us away from sin more and more.

A delightful secret is the link between grace and gratitude. The Greek word – which we render principally as 'grace' – is translated in two principal ways in the New Testament.   When it refers to God's activity it is grace, but when it relates to us it is gratitude.   The lesson is plain: the only appropriate response to grace is gratitude, and all who genuinely experience God's grace in Jesus Christ find instinctively that they must respond with a gratitude which shows itself in a life-style that aims to please God.   When we realise that it is not just everything that we owe to the Lord Jesus, but more than we can ever appreciate, we hate our sins all the more, and every time we are forgiven, we determine all the more strongly to live to please Him.

When a woman taken in the act of adultery was brought to Jesus, He saw through the hypocrisy of her accusers, and He knew the repentance which was in her heart.   She discovered His grace when He said to her, 'I do not condemn you.'   But at the same time, He implied the proper response of gratitude, when He continued, 'Go now and leave your life of sin' (John 8:10,11).

Peter failed the Lord Jesus dreadfully, and denied Him three times.   He could never forget his failure.   But the Lord Jesus came to him with His forgiving and restoring grace at the Sea of Tiberias after His Resurrection.   He showed Peter that he was forgiven but at the same time He reminded him that the proper response to such grace was gratitude shown in caring for His sheep (John 21:15-17).

Sins not sin

Moment by moment we need to know the grace of our Lord Jesus Christ's forgiveness.   The provision is always available to us: that is the clear assurance of the Bible. On our part this calls for the confessing of our *sins* rather than simply the confession of *sin*. The promise is clearly stated: 'If we confess our *sins,* he is faithful and just to forgive us our sins and purify us from all unrighteousness' (1 John 1:9) – and all through the grace of the Lord Jesus Christ. But the stress must be upon the word *sins* rather than *sin*. Sadly, it may not cost my pride and conscience much to say, 'Lord, I have sinned.' But it costs me a lot, and causes me to hate my sin, to confess, 'Lord, I have been proud or jealous or mean' or whatever else my sin has been. To be specific in confessing our sins is what God requires.

We do well to keep short accounts with God. We do not need to wait until the end of the day to confess our sins. In fact, to do so is foolish because unconfessed sin spoils our fellowship with God immediately we sin. We do not need to close our eyes to pray, but just where we are we may run to God and ask for the grace of the Lord Jesus' forgiveness. Honestly sought, it will be generously and completely given. I have in my mind's eye, a young child playing in a garden. It falls over and immediately runs to its parent, perhaps crying. The parent cleans the grazed skin or kisses it better, and off the child goes to continue its activity. As often as we fall we need to run to our heavenly Father in the name of His Son and receive once more the grace of His Son's forgiveness. This is a most precious provision, never to be taken for granted, but to be received thankfully, and responded to with grateful living.

Chapter Three

The Grace of Jesus Christ's presence

To be forgiven by God is to be restored to a right relationship with Him. This explains why in the gospels we find Jesus following up His words of forgiveness with the command 'Go in peace' – literally 'Go into peace' (Luke 7:50). Reconciled to God through Jesus Christ, we are privileged to possess the assurance of His presence.

Jesus Christ's presence is a gift of sheer grace. Sadly, it is a benefit we sometimes take for granted, or simply do not appreciate. If an important dignitary – like a king, queen or president – visited us in our home, we would consider that great condescension, and we would acknowledge that person's grace. Yet how much more gracious and condescending is the presence of Jesus Christ, guaranteed not by our merits but by His grace.

God's intended purpose

The assurance of His presence is something that God has always wanted His people to enjoy. The daily highlight for Adam and Eve in Eden was the cool of day when the Lord God walked in the garden and they enjoyed fellowship with Him (Genesis 3:8). Whatever form that fellowship took, it indicated that God wanted them to take joy in His presence.

The Book of Genesis sums up the godly life of Enoch in a telling phrase when it speaks of his 'walking with God' (Genesis 5:24). Enoch enjoyed God's presence so much that heaven is heaven to him because there he now perfectly enjoys God's presence. Heaven, however, was in Enoch before he was in heaven as he delighted in God's company. The Book of Genesis later outlines Joseph's life, and his difficulties and suffering, but the saving factor was that 'the Lord was with Joseph' (Genesis 39:23).

In the book of Ezra we find expressions describing 'the hand of the Lord' being upon individuals and groups of people (Ezra 7:6,28;8:31).   'The hand of the Lord' is a way of expressing God's presence by His Spirit with people.   We are not told how they discerned this, but they did.   Similarly in the Book of Psalms David and other writers knew this same experience.

Speaking of his determination to set the Lord always before him, David declares, 'Because he is at my right hand, I shall not be shaken' (Psalm 16:8).   The simple expression 'at my right hand' conveys a powerful truth.   If we are right-handed, whenever we feel for something or reach out perhaps for help, we instinctively use our right hand.   David knew that the Lord was always there exactly where and when he needed Him.   In the Shepherd psalm, David recalls the safety and security that his own presence gave to his sheep, and, as one of the Lord's sheep himself, he declares of the Lord, 'Even though I walk through the valley of the shadow of death, I will fear no evil, for you are with me; your rod and your staff they comfort me' (Psalm 23:4). These are no glib words; they are the voice of long experience.

Psalm 73, ascribed to Asaph, confidently expresses the joy of God's presence: 'I am always with you; you hold me by my right hand.   You guide me with your counsel, and afterwards you will take me into glory.   Whom have I in heaven but you?   And earth has nothing I desire besides you.   My flesh and my heart may fail, but God is the strength of my heart and my portion for ever' (Psalm 73:23-24).

Matthew records our Lord Jesus Christ's final promise to His disciples – a promise for all believers at every stage of human history – 'And surely I will be with you always, to the very end of the age' (Matthew 28:20).

A timely presence

The Lord Jesus Christ usually makes His gracious presence known in those key moments when we most need the assurance it gives.   While we know He is with us because of His promises, we do not always feel that He is.   If we did, we would probably take this benefit for granted.   But on those crucial occasions when we need His support, He is able to communicate by His Spirit that He is present – at our right hand.

Samuel Rutherford lay one night in jail in Aberdeen, and he wrote, 'Jesus Christ came to me in my cell last night, and every stone glowed like a ruby.'   David Livingstone said that it was not David Livingstone who walked through Central Africa, it was David Livingstone and Jesus Christ.

One of the apostle Paul's last letters – 2 Timothy – describes how Paul once found that he was very much on his own, and in physical danger.   'No-one came to my support, but everyone deserted me,' he shares with Timothy (4:16).   Yet that statement is wonderfully counterbalanced by another: 'But the Lord stood at my side' (4:17).   Plainly Paul did not see with his physical eyes the Lord standing by him, but Paul was as sure of it as if he had!   Faber put it well in the verse of one of his hymns:

> *'Thrice blest is he to whom is given*
> *The instinct that can tell*
> *That God is on the field when He*
> *Is most invisible.'*

The benefits of Christ's presence

The happy consequences of Christ's presence with us are count-less.   Situations of challenge provide new evidences of its bless-ing, as Acts 4:23-35 illustrates.   Peter and John were instrumental in pointing a man crippled from birth to faith in Jesus.   His heal-ing gave rise to something of an uproar, and Peter and John found themselves brought before the religious authorities, and then forbidden to 'speak or teach at all in the name of Jesus' (Acts 4:18).   The story – to which we shall return in a later chapter – tells how they and their fellow-believers resorted at once to prayer.   What is significant is that we are told that 'much grace was with them all' (Acts 4:33).   We do not need to ask, 'Whose grace?' for every time grace is mentioned in the New Testament it has in view that of the Lord Jesus.   In spite of all the opposition that surrounded them, they were supremely aware of their Lord's presence.

The first consequence was their boldness: they 'spoke the word of God boldly' (Acts 4:31). They did not minimise the seriousness of the threats made to them if they continued to teach and preach God's message, but with their Lord with them they were unafraid, and could take on all opposition! A single Christian with Jesus at his or her side is in the majority! Assured of our Lord's presence with us, we are bold in our witness to Him, overcoming our natural fears and self-consciousness.

The second consequence of Jesus' grace – His presence with them – was the impetus to follow their Lord's example. Christian discipleship demands likeness to Jesus in character and in life – not easy in a world that is likely to treat us as it treated Him or where following His example, for example, may touch our pockets. Having said 'much grace was with them all', Luke goes on to say immediately, 'There were no needy persons among them' (Acts 4:33,34). The significance of that comment must not be missed. When we are in the company of someone whose life and character we respect, we are inevitably influenced by that person's example to behave in the same way. We observe it in the way children behave, spurred on by their peers whom they admire. But how much more is it the case when we keep company with the Lord Jesus Christ! The early Christians found that when His grace was upon them, 'there were no needy persons among them'! Knowing how He showed His grace in becoming poor to make us rich, they found themselves wanting to be generous too.

Never alone

We cannot put into words the benefit and joy of Jesus Christ's presence. It means that we are never alone. Paradoxically perhaps, it is when we experience extreme loneliness that we are most likely as Christian believers to discover His gracious presence. I, like many others, had to do National Service in the 1950s, and was sent into the army. As a very young Christian, I had never left home before for any great length of time, and I was aware of the necessity of being uncompromising from the beginning in professing the Lord Jesus before others. I can remember still the feeling of loneliness on my first night in a barrack room, and the apprehension I had of kneeling at my bed to pray in the presence of dozens of others. But I was not alone! I felt the Lord Jesus' presence as I had never known it before.

The Lord Jesus Christ is always with us. We need to grasp this truth, and to ensure that we do nothing to spoil our experience of it. When His grace is upon us, we have the assurance of His presence.

Chapter Four

The Grace of Jesus Christ's strength

On our own we are weak. No matter how long we have been Christians, we are empty in ourselves of strength to live to please God. Strength to live the Christian life does not come from lengthy experience, but from a daily relationship to God through His Son Jesus Christ.

Grace and strength are sometimes used interchangeably in the New Testament (2 Corinthians 12:9; Philippians 4:13; 1 Timothy 1:12; 2 Timothy 2:1; 4:17; Hebrews 4:16; 1 Peter 4:11). The beauty of this is that when we know we do not deserve a renewal of strength, God grants it because it is gift given not on account of our merit but because of His grace.

Paul's experience

Paul's letters provide frequent testimony to his discovery of the grace of our Lord Jesus Christ's strength, and nowhere more clearly than in his letter to the Philippians when he writes, 'I can do everything through him who gives me strength' (Philippians 4:13). Like every other statement of the Bible, those words must be seen in their context, so that they are not misapplied. Paul was not suggesting that he could do what he liked, and that he could depend upon Jesus Christ's strength to do so. Such an access to strength would be all too dangerous for our fallible wisdom and plans. But what he did assert was that whatever God's will for him was, the grace of Jesus Christ's strength was amply available to enable him to succeed in his obedience to God.

The immediate context of Philippians 4:13 is contentment. Paul wrote from prison – probably in Rome – with his future uncertain, from the human point of view, as well as his material and financial position.   The Philippians, after some delay had sent Paul a gift to help him, for which he was deeply grateful, both to them and to God.   But Paul's difficult circumstances in prison had taught him new lessons about his Saviour's grace and strength: they could get through to him when his fellow Christians could not.   His strength to be content, even if he was in want and hungry, came from his Saviour.   His strength to be unafraid of what the result of his imprisonment might be when he was put on trial came from the same glorious Source.

Multi-coloured needs require comprehensive strength

Our requirements of strength in different areas of life are numberless.   Some we share in common with most other Christians, but there are particular needs we have which others may not possess in exactly the same way.   But the gracious strength of our Saviour is readily available.

We need strength in order to live self-controlled, upright and godly lives.   Our Christian profession has little value in our local communities unless we show in practice we have been delivered from all wickedness, and now endeavour to live to please God.

Self-control calls for self-mastery, whether in terms of our temper, our desires and our resistance of temptation.   Sin is always crouching like a wild animal at the door wanting to seize us.   Uprightness has to do with our relationships with others, demanding that we always deal with people honestly and justly, even if at cost to ourselves.   Godliness has to do with our relationship to God, with the overriding motive to please Him rather than to please ourselves or others.

These three priorities – self-control, uprightness and godliness – are high and demanding standards.   But Jesus Christ's grace provides the strength, for as Paul writes to Titus 'the grace of God that brings salvation has appeared to all men.   It teaches us to say "No" to ungodliness and worldly passions, and to live self-controlled, upright and godly lives in this present age' (Titus 2:11,12).

Strength is required for the exercise of our spiritual gifts. All of us have a gift – or gifts – as members of the body of Christ, which we are to exercise for the common good of the other parts of the body. The more public gifts – which we often consider the most important – are not always the most indispensable. Some of us may have seemingly insignificant gifts which are more important than we appreciate. But whether our gift or gifts are prominent or even secretly exercised, the only way in which they can be effectively employed is 'with the strength God provides' (1 Peter 4:11) – that is to say, the grace of the Lord Jesus Christ's strength.

The danger always exists of trying to exercise our gift in dependence upon ourselves, and upon our own giftedness. If we apparently succeed in our own eyes and those of others, the outcome will be the inflation of our pride. If, however, we exercise our gift in dependence upon Jesus Christ's grace and strength, our aim will be that 'in all things God may be praised through Jesus Christ' (1 Peter 4:11).

We require fresh supplies of strength when trials and suffering come, and at some point in life they are inevitable for the great majority of us. Our Christian faith provides no exemption from the dangers and perils of daily life in a fallen world. Because we are Christians we cannot expect to be excused from illness, disease and pain. On account of being Christians, we may find ourselves the special target of attacks from the enemy of souls, Satan. Job's experience demonstrates that believers may know suffering in which they may prove and honour God. A redeeming factor in all our trials is that the grace of Jesus Christ's strength is always available.

Paul suffered physically through what he describes as 'a thorn in my flesh, a messenger of Satan' (2 Corinthians 12:7). That it was in his 'flesh' indicates it was a physical ailment or disability. We may be glad we do not know what it was, or else we might be inclined to feel that our illness or limiting physical circumstance was greater than his! Paul pleaded with the Lord to remove it (2 Corinthians 12:8), no doubt convinced he would have been able to serve our Lord Jesus Christ better without it.

Perhaps it was a physically limiting circumstance that constantly preoccupied his mind, the reality of which he could not escape even for a day.

The Lord's answer was a surprise at first to Paul. It was a clear and plain 'No'. But a reason was given, for the Lord said to him, 'My grace is sufficient for you, for my power is made perfect in weakness' (2 Corinthians 12:9). That 'No' was an answer to Paul's prayers as much as a 'Yes' would have been. When ill or suffering, it is all too easy – and perhaps natural – for us to be preoccupied with healing. God's answer is often that we are to bear whatever it is, so that we prove the grace of our Saviour's strength. He is as much glorified in the testimony we give through this, as through any healing He might choose to give.

Paul's whole attitude to his physical suffering changed as a consequence: 'Therefore,' he wrote, 'I will boast all the more gladly about my weaknesses so that Christ's power may rest on me. That is why for Christ's sake, I delight in weaknesses, in insults, in hardships, in persecutions, in difficulties. For when I am weak, then I am strong' (2 Corinthians 12:9,10).

Writing to Timothy, who was faced with a variety of challenges and problems as he served the early churches, Paul wrote, 'You, then, my son, be strong in the grace that is in Christ Jesus' (2 Timothy 2:1).

Chapter Five

Grace for Grace
or one blessing after another

No limit can be placed upon the resources of our Lord Jesus Christ's grace. They are endless, boundless and bottomless. Gospel writer John expresses the truth powerfully in the first chapter of his gospel when he writes that out of the fullness of Jesus Christ's grace we have all received 'grace for grace' (Authorised Version) or 'one blessing after another' (New International Version).

No hoarding but using

Our Lord Jesus Christ gives grace upon grace so that each experience of His grace may be followed by another. His purpose is not that we should hoard His grace in preparation for a day when we may perhaps especially need it, but rather that we should prove its inexhaustible fullness daily.

The principle of 'one blessing after another' was powerfully illustrated for me in a simple incident while staying in a small private hotel in Northern Ireland. With others I was there to speak at a week's Convention. Flying from Edinburgh early on the Saturday morning to Belfast, I was glad after a further car journey to arrive in the late afternoon at the hotel. One of the first things I noticed in my bed-room was the welcome sight of an orange, together with a plate, knife and serviette. Having unpacked my things, and being thirsty, I ate my orange. When I returned from church on the Sunday morning, I discovered that my orange had been replaced, and so it was each day as I ate it. Imagine my amusement on the Thursday when a speaker's wife said at the meal table, 'I did enjoy today the orange that was in our room on Saturday.' 'You have had only one orange?' I asked. 'Well, let me count – Saturday, Sunday, Monday, Tuesday, Wednesday, Thursday – I have had six oranges to your one!' The speaker's wife had imagined that one orange was the lot, but I had discovered that as soon as one was eaten, another replaced it. That is like grace! Jesus gives 'grace for grace', 'one blessing after another'. We do not have to store up grace for a future day: His grace is inexhaustible. As often as we need His grace – whether in His forgiveness, His presence or His strength – we are to ask Him for it.

A foretaste

The glorious prospect before us is that even more grace is to be ours when our Lord Jesus Christ is revealed (1 Peter 1:13). If we are amazed now at His kindness, what will it be like when we see Him, and enter into the glorious inheritance He has prepared for us? As the verse added later to John Newton's hymn puts it,

> *'When we've been there a thousand years,*
> *Bright shining as the sun,*
> *We've no less days to sing God's praise*
> *Than when we first begun.'*

Throughout all eternity the riches of our Saviour's grace will amaze us. What we now know is the merest foretaste of what He has in store for us.

The substance of the Christian life

The unfolding of the significance of the grace of the Lord Jesus indicates how we are meant to live as Christians. First, we are to 'walk in the light' as God is in the light (1 John 1:7), and we may do this only as we daily confess our sins and discover afresh the grace of our Saviour's forgiveness.

Secondly, we are to live in the enjoyment of our Lord Jesus' presence. He promises to be with us, and He cannot lie. He is able to reassure us of His presence at those moments when we most require it.

Thirdly, we are to live in the power of the strength He provides. Jesus Christ 'in us' is the secret of the Christian life (Colossians 1:27). We can do anything that God calls us to, whether in character forming, influence, or specific works of service, through Jesus Christ who strengthens by His grace.

Our Saviour's grace is freely available to us. 'He gives us more grace' (James 4:6). If we are too proud to accept or to ask, then it will be denied us. But if we ask, we receive.

We do well to ask ourselves, 'In what areas of my life do I now need the grace of the Lord Jesus?' Is it in forgiveness because sins have not been faced up to and confessed? Is it in the area of knowing His presence and proving His strength? Whatever the need, and no matter how great it may be, ask for His grace! It is there for the asking.

Every time we pray the grace together with understanding, we are requesting, 'May we know the grace of the Lord Jesus' forgiveness, presence and strength.'

What if you are not yet a Christian? This phrase 'The grace of the Lord Jesus Christ' contains important lessons. Your first need – like everyone else's – is forgiveness. Without it no right relationship with God is possible. You cannot earn it, no matter how hard you try. Forgiveness is the gift of God's grace through His Son, the Lord Jesus. It was made possible at Calvary by Jesus' death as the Substitute for sinners, the propitiation for our sins. It is to Jesus Christ that you must come – just as you are. There is no other way.

As you receive His forgiveness, you will quickly discover His presence and His strength. What more could you ask?

Part Two

Chapter Six

The love of God the Father

In this trilogy of blessings which Paul's prayer represents, the grace of our Lord Jesus Christ is followed by the Father's love. Fundamental to our well-being as human beings is the need we all have to be loved. We may not think about it often, but on reflection we know it to be so.

Love and happiness go hand in hand.   The sense of well-being we may know at this moment - or the lack of it - will inevitably be tied up with how secure we feel ourselves to be in our relationships, and in the love of those who are special to us. We cannot overestimate the importance of family and friends. To be unloved is to be unhappy.

The love of our Creator

Contrary to the impression we may often choose to give, we are not self-sufficient: rather we are creatures of an almighty and loving Creator.   Our Creator is our true security; we need the assurance of His love.   If we meet disturbed children, we are usually right in guessing that their backgrounds are insecure and perhaps lacking in the assurance of love.   Exactly the same is true with regard to the disturbed state of human kind.   It is significant that Cain, having murdered his brother Abel, and having received the just punishment for his sin, identified being hidden from God's presence with becoming 'a restless wanderer on the earth' (Genesis 4:14).   Without the security of God's love, we are, as His creatures, restless and often afraid.

God's self-revelation

God has graciously chosen to reveal His love to us.   As the apostle John puts it in his first letter, 'God is love' (1 John 4:8,16).

He is much else besides, but everything about Him is consistent, and in harmony, with love. John also states the complementary truth that 'God is light' (1 John 1:5), a way of expressing God's holiness. But there is nothing contradictory between God's love and holiness. They are in perfect accord.

If we ask the Bible, What is God's supreme attribute or characteristic? the answer is: His goodness. When we say that God is good, we are declaring Him to be all that He as God ought to be. A truth we need to acknowledge about ourselves is that we are not all that we ought to be. But God is! God's love is His acting in the light of His goodness, as too is His holiness.

When we love people we do the very best we can for them. God's love is the perfection of such action: 'For God so loved the world that he gave his one and only Son, that whoever believes in him shall not perish but have eternal life' (John 3:16). Loving the world, God did the very best He could for men and women of the world.

The Father

In John 3:16, as in 2 Corinthians 13:14, it is God the Father of whom we speak. It is the Father who so loved the world that He gave His one and only Son. It is the Father's love for which we pray. John confirms this in his first letter, when he writes, 'We have seen and testify that the Father has sent his Son to be the Saviour of the world' (1 John 4:14).

Our purpose now, therefore, is to understand for what we are asking when we pray, 'The love of God - the Father - be with us.'

Chapter Seven

The knowledge of the Father's love

Christians are described in the New Testament as those who 'are loved by God' (Romans 1:7), 'loved by God the Father' (Jude 1). Wonderful as it is to be loved in human relationships, it is even more glorious to be loved by God.

Plainly God has a concern for the whole of His creation, but it is of Christians in particular of whom it is said that they are 'loved by God'. The explanation is that to be a Christian is to be 'in Christ'. Our Lord Jesus Christ is the Father's beloved Son, and to be united with Him is to receive and enjoy the Father's love for His Son.

God's intention

God's intention is that we should so know His love for us in Christ, that we rely upon it, for, as John writes, 'We know and rely on the love God has for us' (1 John 4:16a). When we are certain that someone loves us, we rely upon that love and show it by our trusting actions. Sure of my wife's love for me, I rely upon it continually. My whole life is influenced both consciously and unconsciously by that loving and assured relationship. So it is to be with our relationship with God.

God's love has been demonstrated, wonderfully, dramatically and finally in the Lord Jesus Christ, in the Father's gift of Him as our Saviour. The New Testament constantly takes us to the Cross to underline the greatness of God's love for us: 'And this is how we know what love is: Jesus Christ laid down his life for us' (1 John 3:16).

The Father's love in giving His Son to be the propitiation for our sins becomes all the more wonderful when we remember that God the Son is the supreme object of the Father's love. First at our Lord's baptism, and then at His Transfiguration, the Father's voice was heard from heaven declaring, 'This is my Son, whom I love; with him I am well pleased' (Matthew 3:17; 17:5). At His Resurrection the Father was likewise affirming, 'This is my Son, the Son whom I love and in whom I delight.' But out of love for us, the Father did not spare His Son but gave Him up for us all (Romans 8:32).

This then is the love we are to know. We are to know all about it, so that we appreciate and understand it as far as it is possible to do so.

What we are to know about God's love

God's love has no regard at all to our merits. God loves because He loves. He loves because He is love. There was, and is, nothing in us as fallen human beings to deserve God's love. As Paul expresses it, 'In love he predestined us to be adopted as his sons through Jesus Christ, in accordance with his pleasure and will - to the praise of his glorious grace, which he has freely given us in the One he loves' (Ephesians 1:4-6). He has 'saved us, not because of righteous things we had done, but because of his mercy' (Titus 3:4).

His love, therefore, is what we may describe as an electing love. He chose us in Christ 'before the creation of the world' to be the objects of His love (Ephesians 1:4,5). The Bible never tries to explain election, but it simply states it. Much as it may puzzle us, our experience confirms its truth. While at the time of our conversion, we may have felt the weight of our personal responsibility to respond to the claims of our Lord Jesus Christ, when we looked back afterwards we became aware of how God had been working in our lives, drawing us to Himself, long before we appreciated it. What our Lord Jesus said to His disciples applies to us, 'You did not choose me, but I chose you' (John 15:16).

God's love is a declared love. When we genuinely love someone, we delight to affirm that love. The Bible is full of proclamations of God's love for His spiritual family. 'I have loved you,' the Lord declares (Malachi 1:2). He delights to state His love so that we may be sure of it.

His love is a faithful and unshakeable love (Psalm 89:24) which He promises to His people (Isaiah 55:3). It does not fluctuate as our moods may do. No uncertainty exists about it. Because it does not depend upon our merits but upon God's faithful character, our sins and failures do not diminish it, much as our consciences may tell us that perhaps they ought. The Father's unshakeable love is beautifully portrayed in the father's love in the story of the returning prodigal son. The father's arms were open, and his acceptance of his son was never in doubt. The whole history of the Jewish people underlines the solid certainty of God's love for His people, in spite of all their spiritual waywardness.

His love is eternal. 'His love endures for ever' is the chorus and testimony of God's people throughout the ages (Ezra 3:11; Psalm 118:1,2,3,29). It is eternal in its dimensions: it has always been directed towards us, and always will be. It was given to us before the beginning of time, and we shall bask in its security and wonders when time as we now know it ceases. What God said to Israel is true of the whole Israel of God, the Church of Jesus Christ, 'I have loved you with an everlasting love; I have drawn you with loving-kindness' (Jeremiah 31:3).

God's love is immense: 'For as high as the heavens are above the earth, so great is his love for those who fear him' (Psalm 103:11). A small boy who had always lived in the country, was taken to the sea for the first time. His immediate response on his first sight of it was to ask, 'Where's the other side?' God's love is vaster than the vastest ocean.

God's love is a Father's love. The enemy of souls, Satan, will try to rob us of our certainty of this truth. God our Father is the perfect Father. When we call God 'Father', we are not saying that God is *like* a Father, but that He is *the* Father. All genuine feelings of fatherhood - and motherhood - in His creatures are reflections of His image in us. While human fatherhood may often be deficient, His never is.

The Lord Jesus teaches us to use this name when we address God: 'This, then, is how you should pray: "Our Father in heaven ..."' (Matthew 6:9).   As our heavenly Father He knows our needs and takes care of them (Matthew 6:32).   We are taught by our Saviour to reason on the basis of God's Fatherhood, using what we may describe as 'the how much more' argument.   'If you, then, though you are evil, know how to give good gifts to your children, how much more will your Father in heaven give good gifts to those who ask him!' (Matthew 7:11).

Our Father's love is a wise love.   He does not give His children anything but good gifts.   That explains some of our seemingly 'unanswered prayers'.   He does not always provide what we want or ask for, but what we need.   One of my young granddaughters was in our home just before Christmas.   As she was leaving I said, 'What do you want for Christmas?'   'An umbrella,' was her reply.   I, rather stupidly, responded, 'What a large one - like your Daddy's golf umbrella?'   'Oh, yes,' she replied!   Her mother did buy her an umbrella, but a dainty one, suitable for a little girl.   So our heavenly Father in His love gives us what is best and appropriate, no matter how foolishly we may sometimes want and ask for the wrong things.

His love is also a chastening love.   As the writer to the Hebrews puts it so forcibly: 'My son, do not make light of the Lord's discipline, and do not lose heart when he rebukes you, because the Lord disciplines those whom he loves, and he punishes everyone he accepts as a son' (Hebrews 12:5,6). Alongside these words we may place those of the Book of Lamentations: 'Though he brings grief, he will show compassion, so great is his unfailing love' (Lamentations 3:22).

The more we get to know ourselves - and that proves to be synonymous with getting to know God more - the more aware we become of our need of God's gracious discipline.   He employs all the varied circumstances of life - its disappointments, heartaches, trials and pain - to make us in character more like His Son, Jesus Christ.   At the time the chastisement is unpleasant, and sometimes extremely painful, but the final purpose is glorious.

His love, therefore, is a love that works everything together for the good of those who love Him, and who have been called according to His purpose (Romans 8:28). That 'good' is not to be read as necessarily immediate good, or material good, but our good in terms of God's glorious purpose to conform us to the likeness of His Son (Romans 8:29).

A paradox

Although it is a love that surpasses knowledge (Ephesians 3:19), we are to know, grasp, and comprehend it! As believers we are to know that God loves us, and that His love surrounds us. His love means that He deals with us as friends - and more than as friends, as His sons and daughters. 'How great is the love the Father has lavished on us, that we should be called children of God' (1 John 3:1).

Nothing grieves our heavenly Father more than that we should doubt His love. As a human father, few things would upset me more than my children doubting my love for them. If I thought that they had even the suspicion of a doubt, I would want to be in touch with them immediately to let them know that I love them. We are loved by God the Father, and He wants us to know it!

Chapter Eight

The assurance and experience of the Father's love

When we pray, 'The love of God be with you' we are asking that we may have the knowledge of God's love firmly fixed in our minds, so that we live our lives relying upon it. But we pray for more than that, since we seek also the assurance and experience of the Father's love.

A key verse is Romans 5:5, where Paul writes, 'God has poured out his love into our hearts by the Holy Spirit, whom he has given us.' 'Poured out' is the same expression used of the Holy Spirit at Pentecost when, according to the prophet Joel's words, God promised that He would 'pour out' His Spirit on all people (Acts 2:17). The verb implies profusion, abundance and overflowing.

The chief blessing

God's love is poured into our hearts by the Holy Spirit. While it is true that the Holy Spirit gives us love for one another, that is not the love that is principally in view here. Rather the focus is upon the Holy Spirit pouring into our hearts an overwhelming awareness of God's love for us. It is not an exaggeration to say that the chief blessing poured out by God with the gift of His Spirit is the sense of His love.

The Holy Spirit's delight is to assure us of the Father's love. Now this is something more than knowing the Father's love. It is knowing, feeling, and being absolutely sure that He loves us. We have in view, therefore, an abundant assurance of the Father's love. It is hard to describe, since it is better felt than explained. But there are moments when we not only know that God loves us, but we feel His delight, pleasure and tenderness to us. We know this sometimes in human relationships. We may have no doubt at all that members of our family love us, but perhaps in a time of crisis, they are unusually demonstrative, and besides knowing their love, we feel it.

When once the Holy Spirit has made God's love overwhelmingly real to us in inward experience, we are bound to think ever afterwards, 'If God loves me like that, and as much as that, He will love me to the end!' This experience is particularly associated with our understanding of the Cross. The Spirit delights to give us fresh views of God's love in His giving up of His Son for our sakes, and we then begin to reason, as Paul did, 'He who did not spare his own Son, but gave him up for us all - how will he not also, along with him, graciously give us all things?' (Romans 8:32). Like the writer of Psalm 63, we have to declare, 'Your love is better than life' (3).

A testimony

Henry Venn was a godly Church of England minister in the eighteenth century. His wife died leaving him with five young children to look after. He was devastated at his loss, as any husband would be. He corresponded with the Countess of Huntingdon, whose appreciation of the importance of being assured of God's love was particularly evident. Although Venn's position was tragic, his letter to her demonstrates the Spirit's ability to pour out into our hearts the assurance of God's love. Venn wrote, 'I am now a living witness of the truth you so strenuously maintain, and of the necessity of that truth in our miserable condition here below. Did I not know the Lord to be mine, were I not certain His heart feels even more love for me than I am able to conceive, were not this evident to me, not by deduction and argument, but by consciousness, by His own light shining in my soul as the sun's doth upon my bodily eyes, into what a deplorable situation should I have been now cast?' It is noteworthy that it was 'not by deduction and argument' that Henry Venn was assured of God's love, but 'by consciousness', by God's own light shining into his soul.

Charles Simeon, the outstanding evangelical preacher in Cambridge around the same period, writes of Romans 5:5: 'This is a blessing which, though not appreciated or understood by those who have never received it, is yet most assuredly enjoyed by many of God's chosen people. We scarcely know how to describe it, because it consists chiefly in an impression on the mind occasioned by manifestations of the love of God to the soul.'

Christian assurance

This inward experience of God's love is the highest form of Christian assurance. It is God saying to us, 'You are mine, and I am yours.' It has been suggested that the greatest characteristic of the greatest saints has been their realisation of God's love, and this has the ring of truth about it as we read Christian biographies. With one voice they declare -

> *'Loved with everlasting love,*
> *Led by grace that love to know;*
> *Spirit, breathing from above,*
> *You have taught me it is so;*
> *O what full and perfect peace,*
> *Joy and wonder all divine!*
> *In a love which cannot cease,*
> *I am His and He is mine.'*
> (G. W. Robinson)

God's love is like the sun. We know that it is always there, and that it shines unceasingly, but there are moments when we look up, as we consciously feel its warmth upon our faces. God's love is always towards us, and it never fails to be directed at us, but there are times when we feel its warmth, so that we look up to Him with gratitude beyond the power of words to express.

God's love is like a fountain. No matter how often we drink from it, it always refreshes. We never come to an end of its flow. When nothing else satisfies, His love quenches our deepest thirst, and consoles us in our greatest troubles.

God's love is like healing medicine, when nothing else will heal. We may suffer loss - as Henry Venn did - and bitter disappointment in human relationships, but in the darkest storm, we may hear God whisper by His Word and His Spirit, 'I love you!' and He quiets us with His love (Zephaniah 3:17).

Certain of God's love, we are more than conquerors, whether we know trouble, hardship, persecution, famine, nakedness or sword (Romans 8:35,37).   Assured of God's love we see everything in a different and better light.   I will not easily forget visiting a young mother in hospital.   I knew she was apprehensive because she was to have an operation similar to one which her mother had undergone with fatal consequences.   But as I entered the ward the day she went into hospital, with the operation to follow the next day, I could see that she was very bright, and soon she shared one of the reasons.   Her son, who was not usually demonstrative, and would leave home for school with scarcely a glance back at his mother as she stood watching him disappear out of sight, on this particular morning had acted differently.   First, he had kissed her 'goodbye'!   Then as he went down the street, he kept looking back, and waving.   At the end of the street, he turned off to school, but suddenly reappeared and waved again.   Previous to this his mother had never doubted his love for her, but today she felt it!   A potentially forbidding day had been transformed by the feeling of being loved.

How much more does the assurance of God's perfect love provide a different perspective on our difficulties and drive out fear (1 John 4:18)!   We see everything in a better and more constructive light.   As Robert Murray M'Cheyne put it, 'There is no rest for the soul like being in the love of God; that is rest.'

If we lack this assurance and experience of the Father's love, we should not hesitate to go to our Father, and ask Him for it. Our priority need sometimes is to feel His everlasting arms about us (Deuteronomy 33:27).   We may cry, in the words of Charles Wesley's hymn,

> *'O Love Divine, how sweet Thou art!*
> *When shall I find my willing heart*
> *All taken up by Thee?*

'God only knows the love of God;
O that it now were shed abroad
In this poor stony heart!'

Such words are associated with times of revival.   When the Spirit comes upon God's people, He sheds God's love abroad in their hearts.

Chapter Nine

The power of the Father's love

In praying, 'The love of God be with us', we ask not only for the knowledge and assurance of the Father's love, but also for its power in our lives. His love is a dynamic force: it does things; it is always active.

Reproduction

The power of the Father's love is that it reproduces itself in the lives of His spiritual children. Even as the moon reflects the sun's light, so we are to reflect God's love in a dark and often loveless world.

His love is an example for us to copy. The love He demonstrated at Calvary is to be shown by us to one another, and then to the world. As John puts it, 'No-one has ever seen God; but if we love one another, God lives in us and his love is made complete in us. We know that we live in him and he in us, because he has given us of his Spirit' (1 John 4:12,13).

God the Father gives His Spirit to live in us, the Spirit who anointed and guided His Son in His earthly ministry. The first evidence and aspect of the Spirit's fruit is love (Galatians 5:22). The person who truly loves is born of God and knows God (1 John 4:7). This recognition mark of a genuine Christian must not be watered down. If we are born into the Father's family, we show the Father's love. If we do not demonstrate that love, then our spiritual birth must be in question.

A powerful love

The power of God's love in us cannot be overestimated. It is patient with people, seeking always to understand them, and their actions.   It is kind in that it tries to find a gentle way of dealing with people.   It looks for a way of being constructive rather than destructive.   It does not envy because it does not begrudge what others enjoy - whether in spiritual gifts, natural abilities or talents.   It does not boast, in that it is more conscious of what others do not have than of what it possesses itself.   It is sensitive to the feelings of others.

God's love reproduced in us is not proud.   It does not consider first its own needs but rather those of others.   It does not rest upon what has been achieved, but looks rather at what still needs to be done.   It is not rude, being conscious neither of class nor position, and treats everyone in the same way.   It is not self-seeking, asking not 'What can I get out of this situation?' but 'What can I give to it?'

This powerful love is not easily angered, and is not touchy. It keeps no record of wrongs.   It is not like a calculator with a memory button.   It avoids deliberate recollection of anything done against it.   It finds no delight in evil but only in good.   It has no ears for gossip, and finds no pleasure in hearing bad things even if they are true.   It always protects, trusts, hopes and perseveres.   It does not stop caring, no matter how many rebuffs it receives, and it persists in believing the best of people, never taking failure as final.   This is the fruit of the Spirit in us, the power of God's love as Paul describes it in 1 Corinthians 13.

1 Corinthians 13 portrays the love that Jesus Christ, the visible image of the invisible God, personified.   Born into the Father's family, we are to become more and more like our heavenly Father, and therefore like His Son.

A love that copes with storms

We are to be rooted and established in the Father's love (Ephesians 3:17), like a tree whose roots make it firm and beyond the possibility of movement.   Where we lived in London, our home was on a corner, with a small stretch of garden alongside the house on both sides of the corner.   Thinking it would be good to get my car off the road, I decided to concrete a small patch of garden on one side of the corner so as to make room for the car. But I had great difficulty in doing so because of a long-established tree at the actual corner itself, which took up a great deal of the available area, and presented a potential hazard to any car reversing into the space. On my day-off, which was a Thursday, I decided to remove the tree. The day ended with the tree still there, and with myself frustrated! I had lopped a number of branches, and removed the top of the tree, but I could not budge the tree at its roots. I buffeted it with everything in my power to remove it but it remained steady.

The following Saturday, I enlisted the help of friends, but try as we might we could not dislodge the tree on account of its well established roots. So far as I know, it is still there! Subsequently I have seen in that tree something of a parable. Our love will often be buffeted in our relationships with others, and not least within the local church. Our fellow Christians may disappoint us, even as we may sadly disappoint them. But that should never mean that we give up on them, or that they give up on us. Even if they fail us, we should not fail them. Like firmly rooted trees in fierce storms, we should remain, rooted and established in love, and loyal to them, no matter what the buffetings. Love is to weather every storm, and God's love in us does. The power of God's love is to be evident in every relationship and in all our church fellowship. We are to abound in love more and more (1 Thessalonians 4:10).

Love's covering power

'Love covers over a multitude of sins' (1 Peter 4:8). I was asked by a group of Chinese Christians in Edinburgh to give a talk on the New Testament's teaching about love. Bearing in mind love's unique ability to cover over sins, I threw out the question, 'Which is the better picture of love covering over sins - the snow falling or the sea coming in and covering the beach? A young Chinese student put up her hand at once with the answer, 'The sea.' And she was right. When snow falls, everyone's garden, for instance, looks the same, and all deficiencies are covered. But, when the snow melts, everything is as it was before. So, sadly, it is with some who say that they forgive others the wrong they have done them.   They appear to show love in forgiving them, but after a time it 'melts' and they remember, and no real forgiveness has been shown.

How different is the sea!   Imagine a busy beach in the summer after a day's activities.   The sand bears many traces of ice-cream papers, the marks of deck-chairs, and the remains of sand-castles.   But in comes the tide.   Slowly, gently, but unrelentingly, the sea covers everything, smooths the sand, removes the debris, and all traces of the day's activity on the beach are gone, and gone for ever, impossible to retrieve.   That is a delightful illustration of the power of God's love in our hearts.   When we forgive, we genuinely forgive.   When we say we forgive, we consistently try to forget.

The secret of obedience

An important aspect of the power of God's love is the obedience to Him it produces.   It is impossible to respond adequately to His love without wholehearted obedience.   At the same time, it is one of the secrets of discovering more of His love: the more we obey our Father the more we open ourselves to further discoveries of His love - and so the process goes on.   This is an application of Jesus' principle that more is given to those who have, and those who have not soon lose whatever they possess (Luke 19:26).   There can be no standing still in the Christian life. Growth in the knowledge of God - and in the practice of love - is the order of the day.

All failures in our obedience to God are failures to appreciate His love for us.   When our eyes are firmly fixed on our heavenly Father's unfailing love we cannot fail to see that His commandments and instructions have our highest good in view. To obey is life; to disobey is folly.

Chapter Ten

Taking stock of our experience of the Father's love

One of the saddest things in Christian experience is to lose our awareness of the knowledge, assurance and power of God's love. The three benefits go together. Our ability to display God's love hinges upon our private and individual consciousness of His love. Losing that, we lose the power to reflect His love.

Identifying the hindrances

There are three principal checks upon our personal awareness of God's love. The first is ignorance or neglect of the Scriptures. It is by means of His Word that God declares His love to us. Of course, He declares much more than that, but His declarations of His love and care are part of the spiritual bread by which our souls are meant to live. When two people are in love, and express their love in writing, they reread each other's letters time and time again to feel the love of the one they love. If we neglect Bible reading, and meditation upon God's Word, it should not surprise us if we find our awareness of His love fading.

The second constraint upon our awareness of God's love is our grieving of the Spirit. As God's children, the Holy Spirit is always with us, for He makes our bodies His temple. As our ever-present Friend, He educates our conscience, prompts us to do what is right, and restrains us when we would do wrong. But by ignoring His promptings, and throwing off His restraint, we grieve Him. Since He is the One who sheds God's love abroad in our hearts, and enables us not only to know but to feel God's love, it should come as no surprise that when we grieve Him we forfeit this aspect of His ministry.

The third limitation upon our awareness of God's love is failure on our part to exercise love to others.   The Bible - and the New Testament in particular - will not allow us to separate love for God from love for our fellow-Christians.   We demonstrate our love for God by our love for one another.   Any cloud on our fellowship with others dims our fellowship with God.   Satan may endeavour to convince us that this is not the case, but he is a liar.   The reason why so many Christians are bitter, hard and unloving - and unaware of the warmth of God's love - is that they have allowed a wrong relationship to continue, and perhaps for so long that they now fail to recognise the original cause of their problem.

Any of these blockages, or a combination of them, can be the cause of our not knowing and feeling God's love to be with us.

A glorious future prospect

The exciting prospect is that God's love is to be experienced by us in its full extent in the life to come.   '"No eye has seen, no ear has heard, no mind has conceived what God has prepared for those who love him"' Paul writes, 'but God has revealed it to us by his Spirit' (1 Corinthians 2:9,10).   Then we shall know as we are known: 'Now we see but a poor reflection as in a mirror; then we shall see face to face' (1 Corinthians 13:12).

All our questions will then be answered, for while not doubting God's love in the difficulties and tragedies of life, we do wonder at times what God's purposes are in sadnesses that He permits to come into our lives.   Dr. William Sangster, a Methodist minister, sought to comfort a man whose two best friends had died within a few days of one another, the parents of five little children.   Dr. Sangster told the story of how as a boy he went away with his friends camping.   At the end of the first week he ran out of money.   So he sent a postcard home to his father asking for help.   Then he met the postman every morning, but no money arrived.   His friends gathered around him, rather like Job's comforters.   They all suggested different reasons for the non-arrival of the money.   One had the brilliant idea - or so he thought - that his father was busy and had forgotten. Dr. Sangster's response was, 'Oh no! That was not the answer. Wherever I was my Dad would never forget me. Never! So they said, "Well, what do you think?" and I said, "I don't know what to think, *but I am going to ask him when I get home*" (Paul Sangster: *Doctor Sangster,* p. 276). When we arrive 'home' all our questions will be answered by our heavenly Father, and the answers will not be a contradiction of His love but a glorious exhibition of it.

Action

We need to be deliberate in our meditation upon God's love. His words and promises are in the Bible for that purpose. They are the declarations of the one true God, the God and Father of our Lord Jesus Christ, who cannot lie. If we keep any kind of prayer diary, it is beneficial to write down verses of Scripture concerning our Father's character, and especially His love, so that they become increasingly familiar to us, and part and parcel of our life.

If we lack the assurance of His love, we should cry to Him for it, for it is the gift of His Spirit. If we being evil, know how to give good gifts to our children, how much more will the Father give the Holy Spirit - and the assurance of His love - to those who ask Him?

We shall be in a position then to prove from experience the power of God's love. There is no human situation of conflict or tension where God's love proves to be impotent. By the power of His love seemingly invincible barriers can be broken down. Was it not His goodness - His love - that brought us, hardened as we were, to repentance?

Perhaps you have never yet discovered the reality of God's love. There is but one place to begin: it is at the Cross of Jesus Christ. There we see God's justice in punishing human sin; and His unspeakable love in allowing His wrath to fall upon His Son standing in the place of sinners. The love God has for sinners now is the love He showed for sinners then! See His love. Be sure of it, and respond to it with repentance towards God and faith in His Son Jesus Christ.   The Father will 'run out' to meet you, as the father did in the story Jesus told of the prodigal son. You will not only know then that God loves you, but you will feel it, and prove its power.

When we pray, 'The love of God be with us', we are asking, 'May we know the Father's love, feel and be assured of it, and display its power in our life.'   'The love of God be with us all!'

Part Three

Chapter Eleven

The fellowship of the Holy Spirit

2 Corinthians 13:14 contains three of the most delightful words of the Christian vocabulary in every language: grace, love and fellowship.

Fellowship is a distinctively Christian word because of the especially important place Christians find fellowship has in their lives. The first Christians discovered this immediately at their new birth on the Day of Pentecost in Jerusalem. Upon their acceptance of the message of the gospel, and their baptism, the first thing we are told is that 'they devoted themselves to the apostles' teaching and to the fellowship, to the breaking of bread and to prayer' (Acts 2:42).

Fellowship is one of the delights flowing from the experience of new birth. Born again into God's family, we discover that a life of fellowship - of eternal fellowship - is before us. In particular, the Christian is to enjoy the fellowship of the Holy Spirit.

A truth

The marked association of fellowship with the Holy Spirit points to a truth that is sometimes overlooked - that is, the personality of God the Holy Spirit. Sometimes we may hear Christians refer to the Holy Spirit as 'it' and that may betray an ignorance of His Personality. The Holy Spirit is a Person, one with the Father and the Son in the Trinity. He is never referred to as 'it' but always as 'He' or 'Him'. It is precisely because He is a Person that He may be grieved and hurt by us (Ephesians 4:30).

Chapter Twelve

The fellowship of the Spirit as Counsellor

When we pray, 'The fellowship of the Holy Spirit be with us', we have in view, first and foremost, His fellowship as our Counsellor. There are many kinds of fellowship from which we profit. I have fellowship with my doctor with reference to my physical well-being. I share with him my state of health, and profit from his counsel. Over the years I have had fellowship with a variety of people who have taught me, with regard to the development of my mind, such as my teachers when was I was young, and in further education as I became older.

We have fellowship with the Holy Spirit with respect to our soul, and the new life we are to live as sons and daughters of God. When Adam and Eve sinned against God, they instantly experienced the penalty of their sin - death. Although physical death came later, spiritual death was immediate. This explains why they proceeded to hide from God, and to feel a sense of shame. God's Spirit - the source of spiritual life in men and women - was taken from them, and they became spiritually 'dead'. Spiritual death is the state into which we are all born. But new birth - regeneration - brings spiritual life to our souls as God's Spirit lives within us.

A very special gift

The Holy Spirit is the gift of the Father and the Son to every believer (John 14:16; 15:26; 16:7). It would be impossible to live the Christian life without Him. He is one of the great gifts of Calvary in the Christian's experience of salvation. In the covenant into which the Father and Son entered - what we may call 'the covenant of redemption' - the Father promised the Son that as a consequence of His Son's death upon the Cross, He would give Him an inheritance of redeemed men and women from every tribe and nation, and that to each He would give the Holy Spirit, who would protect and keep them, so that at the last they would share their Saviour's glory.   But that gift of the Spirit was dependent upon the Saviour's death.   John tells us that Jesus declared at the Feast of Tabernacles in Jerusalem, 'If anyone is thirsty, let him come to me and drink.   Whoever believes in me, as the Scripture has said, streams of living water will flow from within him.'   John explains, 'By this he meant the Spirit, whom those who believed in him were later to receive.   Up to that time the Spirit had not been given, since Jesus had not yet been glorified' (John 7:37-39).

Everyone born of the Spirit may have the assurance that He who has begun His good work in us 'will carry it on to completion until the day of Christ Jesus' (Philippians 21:6).   Our Lord's death guaranteed that benefit for us, and the Holy Spirit makes it an experienced reality.

A unique ministry

The Holy Spirit has a unique ministry in our lives; He does for us what no one else does or can do.   Our Lord Jesus' main teaching about the Holy Spirit was given in His final conversations with His disciples in the upper room, at the time of His betrayal. His particular emphasis was upon the ministry of the Spirit as 'another Counsellor'.   'I will ask the Father,' He said, 'and he will give you another Counsellor to be with you for ever - the Spirit of truth' (John 14:16,17).   The word 'another' is significant, and should not be passed over quickly.   The implication is that the Holy Spirit does for us what the Lord Jesus did for His disciples.   This is crucial for our proper understanding of the Spirit's ministry.

Think of the benefits the Lord Jesus' presence gave to His disciples during those years they shared with Him.   First of all, He instructed them.   They were the special recipients of God's Word and message.   And then He guided, restrained and encouraged them.   Sometimes they needed correction; other times they required encouragement. Whatever help they lacked He gave them. It was the thought of losing these benefits that made them so upset at the prospect of His departure. But their alarm was unnecessary, as it is for us to covet their experience of being with Jesus.

The Holy Spirit is 'another Counsellor'. A counsellor is literally someone who is called to one's side, or to one's aid, able to give the assistance that is urgently required. The Holy Spirit is our resident Strengthener and Comforter. His is not the comfort of someone who simply says, 'There, there, I understand' and can do no more; rather His is the comfort which strengthens, sustains and always shows the way forward. He is always with us. Jesus promised, 'He will be with you for ever' (John 14:16). He lives with us, and is in us (John 14:17); our bodies have become His temples.

He does for us all that the Lord Jesus did for His disciples and apostles when He was physically present with them. As the Spirit of truth (John 14:17), He teaches us. He always tells us the truth, and encourages us to face up to the truth, and to be truthful. That can be painful, yet necessary, if we are to grow in our knowledge of God. He guides us into all truth (John 16:13), using as His main instrument the Bible, the fruit of His inspiration.

He reminds us of what He has already taught us, and He can give us amazing 'recall' of what we may have learned many years before. In particular, He testifies to us about the Lord Jesus Christ, the ministry in which He most delights (John 15:26). He brings glory to the Lord Jesus by taking what is His and making it known to us (John 16:15). All that belongs to the Father belongs to His Son, and that is why the Spirit takes what is Jesus' and discloses it to us.

The Holy Spirit is the divine Executor, in that He guides us through the spiritual inheritance God has given us in His Son. The Spirit shows us how wonderful it is to be joint-heirs with Christ. He shows us one treasure after another. Whenever we may be tempted to wish that we had been with the disciples in their three years with Jesus, we should remember His words to them, 'It is for your good that I am going away. Unless I go away, the Counsellor will not come to you' (John 16:7). Jesus did go away - via the Cross, the Resurrection and the Ascension - and His Spirit has come, 'another Counsellor'.

Invisible yet powerful

One of the special promises Jesus made to His disciples was of His peace: 'Peace I leave with you; my peace I give you. I do not give as the world gives. Do not let your hearts be troubled and do not be afraid' (John 14:27). By His ministry as the Counsellor, the Holy Spirit brings Jesus' peace to us, a peace which transcends all understanding. His counselling, strengthening and comforting ministry is invisible, yet powerful - in fact, almighty. It penetrates every obstacle and overcomes all barriers.

Luke records how Peter was put in prison by King Herod, part of a plan to persecute the church. 'He had James, the brother of John, put to death with the sword' (Acts 12:2). Peter was under close arrest, with four squads of four soldiers each guarding him, awaiting trial. The church realised his danger in the light of what had happened to James. The night before Peter was due to be brought to trial, the church in Jerusalem arranged an all-night prayer meeting. But what was Peter doing? 'Peter was sleeping' (Acts 12:6)! The Holy Spirit can communicate the Lord Jesus' peace to us when no one else can be in touch with us.

The varying nature of our circumstances presents no problem to the Spirit. He comes alongside when we are weak and overwhelmed, and shares our burden until we consciously and effectively cast it upon God. He is the God-given answer to our experiences of desolation and loneliness, for He never leaves us.

An example of the Spirit's ministry

The Holy Spirit's fellowship as the Counsellor is illustrated in the description the Book of Acts gives of Stephen's martyrdom. Significantly, the first thing we are told about Stephen is that he was 'full of the Holy Spirit' (Acts 7:55). Full of the Spirit, Stephen knew the Spirit to the full as his Counsellor.

The Spirit's help is discernable in practically every statement Luke makes. First, the Spirit enabled Stephen to look up to heaven and to see the glory of God rather than to look around him (Acts 7:55). The temptation to focus upon his persecutors and the stones they were about to throw at him must have been great; but instead he looked up. The Holy Spirit always encourages us to look up, to see our circumstances in the light of the One upon whom our eyes are to be focused, to turn our eyes upon Jesus.

Secondly, he saw Jesus standing at the right hand of God. 'Look,' he cried, 'I see heaven open and the Son of Man standing at the right hand of God' (Acts 7:56). This is the only occasion in the New Testament that Jesus is said to be standing at the right hand of God; the picture is usually of His sitting. But Stephen saw his Lord standing ready to receive him into glory. But it was not with his physical eyes that Stephen saw his Lord. Filled with the Spirit, the Spirit enabled him to see what the human eye could not see, and how that glimpse of his Saviour encouraged Stephen!

Thirdly, the Holy Spirit strengthened Stephen to walk in Jesus' footsteps in spite of the intensity and barbarity of his suffering. 'While they were stoning him, Stephen prayed, "Lord Jesus, receive my spirit." Then he fell on his knees and cried out, "Lord, do not hold this sin against them." Even as his Lord had committed His spirit to His Father, and had prayed for those who crucified Him, Stephen did the same, and his secret was the invisible ministry of the Spirit, the Counsellor, with whom Stephen was filled. The Holy Spirit's counsel is always to make us aware of our oneness with the Lord Jesus Christ, and the ability He can give to walk in Jesus' footsteps.

When we pray, 'The fellowship of the Holy Spirit be with us,' we are praying for His fellowship as our Counsellor.

Chapter Thirteen

The fellowship of the Spirit's intercession

A n essential aspect of the Holy Spirit's fellowship is His teaching us to pray. As I reflect upon my own experience of becoming a Christian - although a long time ago now - I can remember still how instinctive it was to pray as a son to a Father, without anyone having to tell me that this relationship to God was now possible. When Saul - whom we know better as Paul - was converted, Ananias, a Damascus Christian, was told by the Lord Jesus to go to him as a Christian brother. Ananias was understandably a little reluctant in view of Saul's persecuting activities. But his Lord's reassurance to him was 'he is praying' (Acts 9:11). As a baby cries when it is born, so a new-born believer cries to God in prayer. It is one of the many evidences of new birth.

The school of prayer

The Holy Spirit is the headmaster of God's school of prayer. It is a school in which we all commence as beginners, and from which we never graduate, no matter how far up the school we get. The Holy Spirit instructs us from the Scriptures He Himself has inspired that the throne of God, which once we rightly feared as a throne of judgment, has now become a throne of grace - where we may find God's mercy and grace to help in our times of need (Hebrews 4:16). He teaches us the wisdom of making our decisions at God's throne. As we pour out our desires to God, as children to our Heavenly Father, God confirms those that are right by the peace the Spirit communicates, and puts aside those that are wrong, or not the best.

His fellowship in prayer

The Holy Spirit prompts us to pray.   If we pause a moment and think about prayer, we will know within our hearts the prompting of the Spirit, who tells us, as our Saviour did His disciples, that we should always pray (Luke 18:1).   As we go about our daily work, people and situations may frequently come forcibly to mind, and experience shows in retrospect that these are often promptings of the Spirit to engage in intercession for others.

Romans 8:26 is a key statement: 'The Spirit helps us in our weakness.   We do not know what we ought to pray, but the Spirit himself intercedes for us with groans that words cannot express.'   The Spirit helps us: His intercession is made not as our substitute but as our Helper.   He helps us to recognise our need, and to turn our desires into longings which God delights to answer.

By His presence within us, He influences our prayers, and points us in the right direction in our requests.   What is more, when we find it difficult to put into words what we feel, He interprets our inarticulate groans and transforms them into effective prayer.   He stirs up our desires for what is right and in accord with God's will.   That is implied in His title 'the Counsellor'.   One way in which this term was used in the first century was of an advocate in a court of justice, who instructed his client in what to say.   The Holy Spirit puts words and pleas into our mouths, not as His requests, but as ours.

So often as we read the Bible, or hear it preached, we find our longings stirred for God's will to be done in our own lives and the lives of others.   As the Holy Spirit excites our feelings by such means, He also enables us to give them expression in the right manner.   He intercedes in and for us.   He does this, however, only as we ourselves pray.   His intercession is not a substitute for our prayers, but an activity consequent upon, and parallel with, ours.

Every prompting to pray should be responded to, no matter how helpless we may feel sometimes in knowing how to pray. We may make the simple yet powerful cry, 'Lord, help me!' and the Holy Spirit will turn that prayer into a specific request for the precise help we require.

The fellowship of the Spirit in practice

We find an illustration of the fellowship of the Spirit's intercession in Acts 4:23-31. Peter and John gave witness to Jesus' authority in the healing of a man crippled from birth who sat at the temple gate called Beautiful. Such a commotion followed, as they proclaimed the gospel to the astounded witnesses of this miracle, that Peter and John were arrested and brought before the Jewish authorities. The outcome was they were threatened and commanded not to speak any longer in Jesus' name. It is worth considering what our own reaction would have been to such an instruction. I am tempted to think that we might have been inclined to have called a conference or a committee meeting!

The Holy Spirit prompted them to pray as the first thing they did. We read, 'On their release, Peter and John went back to their own people and reported all that the chief priests and elders had said to them. When they heard this, they raised their voices together in prayer to God' (Acts 4:23,24). The Holy Spirit teaches us to pray as our immediate response to challenges to our obedience. What a lot of time we may waste in talking about spiritual battles and problems rather than praying about them!

Secondly, the Holy Spirit moved them to raise 'their voices together in prayer' (Acts 4:24). He is the inspirer of corporate prayer as of personal and private prayer. No Spirit-filled Christian neglects praying with others. Particular promises and blessings are attached to united prayer (2 Chronicles 7:14; Matthew 18:19,20; James 5:14,15).

Thirdly, the Holy Spirit brought to their minds Scriptures to guide their prayers and upon which they should be based. ' "Sovereign Lord," they said, "you made the heaven and the earth and the sea, and everything in them. You spoke by the Holy Spirit through the mouth of your servant, our father David: 'Why do the nations rage and the peoples plot in vain? The kings of the earth take their stand and the rulers stand together against the Lord and against his Anointed One.' Indeed Herod and Pontius Pilate met together with the Gentiles and the people of Israel in this city to conspire against your holy servant Jesus, whom you anointed. They did what your power and will had decided beforehand should happen"' (Acts 4:24-28).

They did not possess the ready access we have to copies of the Scriptures, but the Spirit brought to their minds the most appropriate psalm to their situation - Psalm 2. Psalm 2 sets forth God's purpose of giving His Son an inheritance among the nations, and His perfect sovereignty over all the foolish opposition of human authorities to His purpose. The psalm was tellingly relevant to their circumstances. The Holy Spirit reminded them of God as Sovereign, Lord, Creator, Inspirer of Scripture and the Giver of the Messiah. What confidence and boldness in prayer this inspired!

Fourthly, the Spirit enabled them to ask for grace to be obedient to the Lord Jesus' commission to preach the good news, whatever the opposition. 'Now, Lord, consider their threats and enable your servants to speak your word with great boldness. Stretch out your hand to heal and perform miraculous signs and wonders through the name of your holy servant Jesus' (Acts 4:29,30). They did not ask for the opposition to cease, or for their path to be made easier. Rather they prayed for grace to do what their Lord had commanded. Such prayer can never go unanswered. The Holy Spirit stirred them up to pray prayers of faith - and such prayers please God (Hebrews 11:6). As Luke records, 'After they prayed, the place where they were meeting was shaken. And they were all filled with the Holy Spirit and spoke the word of God boldly' (Acts 4:31).

We are never wiser than when we pray. And when we pray, we are never more certain of help than when we ask for the Holy Spirit's fellowship.

Chapter Fourteen

The fellowship into which the Spirit would bring us

The earnest desire of God the Holy Spirit is to encourage our living and active fellowship with the Father and the Son. 'Our fellowship' John declares, 'is with the Father and with his Son, Jesus Christ' (1 John 1:3). If we ask how this comes about in human experience, the answer is through the gracious fellowship of the Spirit. He delights to make real our personal fellowship with the Father and the Son.

The key importance of our obedience

Since obedience is the key to living in fellowship with the Father and the Son, the Spirit's constant encouragement to us is to obey God's Word. The greatest obstacle to our fellowship with God is disobedience - whether deliberate or unconscious - on account of neglect of God's Word.

The Lord Jesus made two remarkable promises about fellowship with Himself and His Father, and both are found in John 14: 'Whoever has my commands and obeys them, he is the one who loves me. He who loves me will be loved by my Father, and I too will love him and show myself to him ... If anyone loves me, he will obey my teaching. My Father will love him, and we will come to him and make our home with him' (John 14:21,23).

I cannot think of anything more wonderful than Jesus showing Himself to my soul, and the Father and the Son making their home with me. Both of these unsurpassed blessings imparted by the Spirit are dependent upon our love for Jesus Christ expressed in obedience - obedience to His commands and teaching. In the light of this we can understand why the Holy Spirit causes us to be increasingly sensitive to disobedience. At the same time He creates within us a hunger for the enjoyment of the Father's and the Son's making their home with us, and the Lord Jesus showing His glory to us.

Where there's a will there's a way

It is the Holy Spirit who stirs us up to seek fellowship with God, and who blesses us through it.   Isobel Kuhn, a missionary in China, went through a difficult experience as a young school teacher in Vancouver, Canada.   The house in which she stayed was noisy, and she found it hard to keep her prayer times. Others in the house played cards, danced, and had what they called a good time until long past midnight.   She found she could not pray with those noises in her ears.   To get up early was not productive as, once up, her mind rushed on to her school-teaching, which she was not finding easy.

At last she hit on the plan of asking the Lord to wake her up around two o'clock in the morning when the house had settled down to quiet, and then to arise for an hour's prayer and Bible study.   This is what she wrote, 'This worked wonders.   Always a sleepy-head, it was wonderful to me to be awakened each morning, as I was, and in the quiet of that still hour Christ became so real to me that often I felt I could have touched Him, if I but put out my hand.   It was learning ... "the awareness of His presence".   It satisfied me as nothing on earth had ever done.   It filled me with a joy of communion that is inexpressible.   I learned fellowship with Christ, living person to person fellowship which henceforth became dearer to me than ought else in life to me.'

It would be foolish to suggest that we should likewise get up in the middle of the night.   However it is the Holy Spirit who shows us, whatever our circumstances, how we can overcome difficulties in finding time for fellowship with God.   He may show the busy and often harassed young mother that her best time to pray is when her baby or toddler falls asleep, irrespective of when in the day that may be.   He may show the working father who finds quiet at home difficult to obtain at the beginning of the day that he may best be alone with God by getting into the office early before others arrive or going into a city church at lunchtime. The Spirit always shows us the way if we have the will. He teaches us the priority and preciousness of our fellowship with God.

Fellowship with other Christians

Not only does the Spirit bring us into fellowship with the Father and the Son, but He also brings us into fellowship with other Christian believers. He creates a fellowship among all who are 'in Christ', a fellowship which breaks down human barriers, whether of age, sex, colour, background or gifts. He did this at Pentecost, and we have the record of it in Acts 2:42-47 - an example of what He continues to do.

He brings us into the fellowship of those who listen to God's Word and obey it. In the Scriptures - both in their reading and preaching - we hear the voice of our Shepherd, the Lord Jesus. When the Scriptures speak, our Saviour speaks. We will discover that the best fellowship we know as Christians springs from sharing the Bible together.

He brings us into the fellowship of those who love the Lord Jesus and who delight to remember His death at His Table. As we share in a common loaf, we remember we are one body. Members of the same spiritual family, the Spirit makes us sensitive to anything that spoils our relationship with other Christians in order that we may put it right.

He teaches us the fellowship of prayer together. We will find deep fellowship in praying together, for others, and for one another. In ordinary everyday experience, we recognise that to share a burden is to lessen it. But to share in prayer together is to cast our complete burden upon the Lord. Through one another's prayers we will be encouraged, and sometimes discover God's guidance.

He encourages us to practise sharing in the most practical ways. The needs of our brothers and sisters will be laid upon our heart. Sometimes we will give a gift or share something we possess in a visible way; on other occasions, we will share with them without their knowing the source.

The Holy Spirit enables us to discover the unity of God's people through the bond of peace.   He will make us peace-makers, anxious for the well-being of God's people and the honour of Jesus' name.   In particular, the Spirit teaches us to love one another, and the better our love, the stronger our fellowship.

The greater and deeper our fellowship is with the Father and the Son the greater and deeper it is with one another.   They are like two sides of one coin.   We may at first think it difficult to evaluate our fellowship with God, and to know how close it is. If, however, we ask ourselves, 'How close is my fellowship with my fellow-believers?' we have in the answer more than a clue to the reality of our fellowship with the Father and the Son by the Holy Spirit.

Chapter Fifteen

The tragedy of grieving the Spirit

The Holy Spirit is the only Person who can make our fellowship with the Father and the Son a daily reality. He is the God-given Guardian of our relationship with God.

Quenching and grieving the Spirit

Sadly, we may quench and grieve the Spirit. We quench Him by doing what we know displeases Him, by resisting His ministry, and not least as He speaks to us through the ministry of those He raises up to teach us.

We grieve Him by not looking to Him for His counselling ministry. When difficulties come, we may choose to run to everyone else, telephoning perhaps all our friends and pouring out our troubles, with not a thought of calling alongside our Counsellor.

We grieve Him by not seeking His assistance in prayer. All of us find difficulty at times in this area - and on occasions, acute difficulty. But they are probably the times when we most need to pray! The answer is to call upon our Helper. But if we fail to do so, we grieve Him.

We grieve Him by not living in fellowship with God and with members of His family. The two go together. Since the wonder of the life to come is enjoying Him for ever, the greatest blessing of this present life is the anticipation of that wonderful prospect as we enjoy fellowship with God and His people. All believers know in their hearts that time spent with God is time well spent, and that we owe our fellow-Christians some of our time too. To ignore that knowledge is to grieve the Spirit.

We grieve the Spirit by encouraging sinful affections. This is a private and secret matter, known usually only to God and ourselves. Before sin ever surfaces in action it finds a place in heart and inclinations. We cannot help many temptations coming to us, but we can avoid their establishing themselves in our thoughts. To give them room is to grieve the Spirit.

We grieve the Spirit by despising His Word and its preaching. To read the Bible in a careless and offhand manner is disrespectful to its Author. To despise the preaching of His Word because we do not like the personality of the preacher or because we look down upon his ability to communicate may be to shut our ears to the voice of our Master. That grieves the Spirit.

We grieve the Spirit by committing sins we might have avoided. Only we - and God - may know how much we play with temptation.   God is compassionate with us when we fall into sin, with no desire to do so. But the Spirit is grieved when we willingly compromise.

We grieve the Spirit by doing things in our own strength. The best of gifts, and the most marked abilities have no spiritual power when they are exercised in self-dependence.   The strength to accomplish anything effectively for God comes from His Spirit.   To fail to look to Him for power not only makes our service fruitless but it is grieving to the Spirit.

We grieve the Spirit by not doing our service or duty well. How easy it is to be half-hearted while apparently, to others, we appear completely committed.   We cannot deceive the Holy Spirit.   His desire is that we should do whatever we do wholeheartedly, as to the Lord Jesus Himself.   To serve and to perform our duties in a manner unworthy of the Master we profess to serve, grieves Him, especially as His help is always available as we honestly seek it.

We grieve the Spirit by failing to recognise His working in the lives of others.   Filled with the Spirit we are not quick to criticise, but speedy to commend.   When we point the finger at other believers' shortcomings we may be failing to see what the

Holy Spirit has achieved, and is still doing, in their lives, and this grieves Him. The indwelling of the Spirit is synonymous with love dwelling in us.

Our Counsellor and Intercessor is our Friend. How tragic to grieve and limit Him! That can be one of our major sins, and sins of the Church. If so, it needs to be put right. As Faber wisely puts it in one of his hymns, 'Be docile to thine unseen Guide, love Him as He loves thee.'

When we pray, 'May we know the fellowship of the Holy Spirit,' we are asking, 'May we know His ministry as Counsellor, the benefit of His intercession, and the fellowship into which He would bring us with God the Father, God the Son, and with all His people.'

This fellowship may as yet be strange and unknown to some. It was to all of us at one time. There is guidance in this familiar prayer for those who do not yet possess this heavenly Guest and His fellowship. Those who know the fellowship of the Spirit know first the love of God the Father and the grace of God the Son.

See the Father's love in giving His Son for sinners. Understand the Saviour's grace in becoming poor that we might become rich, in dying that we might be pardoned and accepted into God's family. Respond to the Father's love and cast yourself upon the Saviour's grace, and you will discover the fellowship of the Spirit.

Chapter Sixteen

Conclusion

Putting the trilogy of blessings together

'**M**ay the grace of the Lord Jesus Christ, and the love of God, and the fellowship of the Holy Spirit be with you all.' While these words occur but once, they are among the most well-known and popular words of the New Testament. They are probably more significant than we might at first imagine. We have looked at each part separately but it is important to consider them together.

The Christian faith in essence

The words of this prayer provide a summary of the Christian faith for they remind us that the doctrine of the Trinity is the foundation of all that God has revealed and of all that we believe. Since these words are a prayer, and we are taught to pray to God alone, the Personality and Deity of each Person of the Trinity is implied. We address the Lord Jesus for His grace, the Father for His love, and the Holy Spirit for His fellowship. The three Persons equally are the source of grace and blessing to us.

The Christian faith is all about the grace of our Lord Jesus by which we are saved. It is all about the love of God the Father to which we respond. It is all about the experience of the fellowship of the Holy Spirit in everyday life.

An order true to experience

As we ponder the sequence of these three blessings in what we call 'the grace' we have an order that is true to the experience of most of us. It is not always followed, but more often than not it

is.   Our discovery of God begins with the discovery of the grace
of the Lord Jesus Christ.   When we begin to seek after God, we
soon learn how totally different He is from us, and how completely unworthy we are either to find Him or to approach Him.
The only solution is God's grace, and that is precisely what is
offered us in Jesus Christ.

Discovering the truth about Jesus Christ's grace, we are led
on to believe in God's love, and to rely upon it.   As we do so
we find ourselves knowing the fellowship into which His Spirit
brings us, both with God and His people.   The Lord Jesus
Christ's grace is the door through which we enter to understand
God's love, and then to discover fellowship with God by His
Spirit.

A profound mystery

We stand on holy ground because we consider a profound mys-
tery.   Our salvation is a Trinitarian salvation.   The Father, the
First Person of the Trinity, is revealed as the One who initiates all
things, who chooses a people to save and His Son to save them,
and who plans a way of salvation consistent with His holy character.

The Son, the Second Person of the Trinity, perfectly reflects
and embodies in Himself the Father's nature and mind, and came
forth from the Father to do His will by dying to redeem sinners.

The Holy Spirit, the Third Person of the Trinity, proceeds
from the First and the Second as their Executive, conveying to
God's chosen people the salvation which God the Son secured
for them.   All three Persons actively fulfil a common purpose of
love to unlovely men and women like ourselves.   All three give
distinct gifts of their generosity and abundance to redeemed sinners, and all three, therefore, should be clearly acknowledged by
God's people in their faith and obedience.

It is through the grace of the Lord Jesus that we come to
know the Father's love, for it is the Father's grace that He
reveals.   It is through the Father's love that we have entered into
the grace of the Lord Jesus.   The Spirit - and the fellowship into
which He brings us - are the gift of the Father and the Son.

The special ministry of the Spirit now

A truth that emerges strongly the more we meditate upon the words of 'the grace' is the unique ministry the Holy Spirit exercises at this time. He it is who teaches us the grace of the Lord Jesus and the love of the Father. He it is who woos us to repentance and faith by showing us our Saviour's grace and the Father's love. When we first understood our need of the Lord Jesus' grace in dying for us, and our utter dependence upon the Father's love for lost sinners, it was the Spirit who taught us.

The Holy Spirit comforts us in all our trials and difficulties by acquainting us afresh, and in new ways, with the riches of the Lord Jesus' grace and the unfathomable depths of God our Father's love. The benefits the Lord Jesus and the Father want and purpose to give come by the Spirit.

When the Lord Jesus' forgiveness, presence and strength are made real to us, it is the Spirit who does this. When the assurance of God's love floods our heart, it is the Spirit's gracious activity (Romans 5:5). He makes us knowledgeable about God's love, conscious of it, and aware of its power. He conveys a delightful persuasion of God's love for us, so that we echo both the words and feelings of Paul, 'I am convinced that neither death nor life, neither angels nor demons, neither the present nor the future, nor any powers, neither height nor depth, nor anything else in all creation, will be able to separate us from the love of God that is in Christ Jesus our Lord' (Romans 8:38-39).

A truth of which to lay hold

As we consider this very special ministry of the Spirit, we are made to realise the priority of the fellowship with God into which the Spirit would lead us. Fellowship with God is a relationship of friendship between God and ourselves, achieved by God Himself, who, in His love and grace, has taken all the initiative in making it possible. It is a relationship in which we receive from, and respond to, all three Persons of the Trinity.

Our fellowship with God the Father and God the Son consists in our possessing the Holy Spirit who is their Spirit. All the fellowship we have with God is by the Spirit.   As we read the gospel records we see how that the communion that our Lord Jesus had as a man with God during His earthly life was by the Holy Spirit (e.g. Luke 10:21).   So too the fellowship God has with us, and we with Him, is by the same Spirit.   The Spirit is the bond of union between the Lord Jesus and us, and the Father and us.   God communicates Himself to us by His Spirit, and we communicate with Him in return by His Spirit who now lives within us.   Everything God accomplishes now in us He does by His Spirit, and we are enabled to do what God wants us to do day by day by His Spirit's enabling power.

Rich toward God

We have to conclude that we are rich beyond measure!   Each of these blessings - the grace of the Lord Jesus, the love of the Father, and the fellowship of the Spirit - is unique.   Knowing them, we cannot imagine where we would be, and what life would be like, without them.

Without the grace of the Lord Jesus Christ we would be dead in transgressions and sins.   There is no other source of grace, and no substitute for His grace.   Without the love of God, we would have no salvation, and no Saviour; instead, we would be in a state of perpetual enmity against God, with all the inevitable consequences of judgment and hell.   Without the fellowship of the Spirit, we would have no living experience of God.   We should meditate frequently, therefore, on these benefits, and most of all on God - Father, Son and Holy Spirit - the source of them.

Benefits and blessings for which to pray

We must not overlook the simple yet profound truth that these are benefits and blessings for which we should pray.   The words of 2 Corinthians 13:14 are a prayer, and when we use them together we are praying that we might all know them in their fullness.

This trilogy of blessings sets before us benefits God wants to give us on a daily and moment by moment basis. They are gifts we are intended to enjoy. They are a foretaste of heaven.

Every time this prayer is prayed we should strive to enter into what we are asking to the very full. Remember it highlights the glorious benefits of salvation we are to know now. We cannot pray for greater blessings upon ourselves or others than the petitions this prayer expresses. John Newton, who wrote, 'Amazing grace, how sweet the sound!' clearly felt this, for he composed a hymn for his congregation at Olney based on this prayer -

> *'May the grace of Christ our Saviour,*
> *And the Father's boundless love,*
> *With the Holy Spirit's favour,*
> *Rest upon us from above.*

> *'Then may we abide in union*
> *With each other and the Lord;*
> *And possess in sweet communion,*
> *Joys which earth cannot afford.'*